The Black Cr

Martin Black

OMNIBUS PRESS
LONDON · NEW YORK · SYDNEY

ISBN: 0.7119.3214.X
Order No: OP 47163

Edited by Chris Charlesworth
Cover & Book designed by 4i Limited
Picture research by David Brolan

Exclusive Distributors
Book Sales Limited,
8/9 Frith Street,
London W1V 5TZ, UK.

Music Sales Corporation,
225 Park Avenue South,
New York, NY 10003, USA.

Music Sales Pty Limited,
120 Rothschild Avenue,
Rosebery, NSW 2018, Australia.

To the Music Trade only:
Music Sales Limited,
8/9, Frith Street,
London W1V 5TZ, UK.

Photo credits:
Front and back cover: George Chin; David Anderson/SIN: 20c, 36tr, 37b, 56b: Edie Baskin: 62t; Richard Bellia: 4/5; Larry Busacca/Retna: 61t; Chris Carroll/Retna: 63: George Chin: 17(x3), 18(x2), 19, 22(x3), 27, 28b, 29b, 34, 38, 39tr, 42t, 51, 53, 54b, 56c, 57b, 59, 60t&b, 61b; Famous: 55; Frederick/SIN: 8/9, 12/13, 14/15, 15, 16, 25, 42/43, 50; Ken Freidman/Retna: 8t; Gary Gershoff/Retna: 36b; Van Iperan/Retna: 31; Tim Jarvis/Retna: 10b, 26tc, 58b; London Features International: 10t, 11t&b, 13, 20t, 25(inset), 28t, 29t, 37t, 54t, 56t, 58l, 59b, 61br, 62b; Eddie Malluck/Retna: 6t&b, 7(x3), 43b; Robert Matheu/Retna: 33t, 58t; Gordon Milne/Mergemeet: 21, 26b; Tony Mottram/Retna: 2/3, 8b, 26b & tl&r, 36tl, 48, 49, 51b, 61c; Cora O'Keefe: 24, 32/33, 40/41, 45t&b; Michael Putland/Retna: 1, 14t&b, 50b; Retna: 46/47; Mary Scanlon/SIN: 24tr; Mike Seliger/Retna: 23, 41b; Ed Sirrs/Retna: 22tr, 30, 35tl, 39tl, 64; Paul Slattery/Retna: 35b; John Soares/Retna: 19t, 35c, 39b, 57t; Chris Taylor/Retna: 2bl, 20b.

Every effort has been made to trace the copyright holders of the photographs in this book but one or two were unreachable. We would be grateful if the photographers concerned would contact us.

Printed by:
Scotprint, Musselburgh, Edinburgh.

A catalogue record for this book is available from the British Library.

The Black Crowes

"We're young and we're pissed off. The Black Crowes are a gut reaction."
Chris Robinson, The Black Crowes

"The Revolution will not be televised," proclaimed the proto-rap group the Last Poets at the end of the Sixties. They were wrong. According to the 1992 handbook of rock'n'roll stardom, the Revolution will not only be televised (via satellite to the world), but it'll also be sponsored by Coca-Cola.

The canyon between the ideal of rock as some primeval force of youthful rebellion, and the reality of multi-national corporations financing carefully orchestrated, million-dollar world tours, must have struck everyone for whom the music is still more important than the media manipulation. That same gulf sparked the birth of the punk movement, which spent a heady five minutes in open revolt against the system before sliding into the very same career moves adopted by the dinosaur supergroups they once despised so much: stadium gigs and greatest hits albums, grand reunion tours and corporate sponsorship.

Tour sponsorship is a particularly sore point. Even the most outrageous rock stars have occasionally lent their names to commercial products; usually they were flattered and amused to be asked, and it's doubtful if there is a band of any stature in the world who hasn't accepted a free guitar, amp or drum-kit in exchange for a plug for quality hardware like Gibson, Marshall or Premier on their album sleeve. But by the mid-Eighties, sponsorship suddenly meant something far beyond this, and even beyond The Rolling Stones vamping their way through a breakfast cereal commercial, or The Jefferson Airplane turning Levi's ads into acid-rock

financed a stadium tour by an Elton John or Michael Jackson — or ZZ Top — the product was being sold just as hard as the band. The concession stands offered no choice: you sank another Pepsi or you dehydrated. The concert programme, its price inflated to soak the ego of the artist, was filled with shots of another rock superstar grinning inanely as he prepared to down a glass of some sweet, lifeless, cloying confection. Worst of all, where the artist and music should be supreme, huge banners displayed the corporate logo of the sponsors. Once, product advertising used to be a profitable sideline. In the age of tour sponsorship, the art was overshadowed by the advert.

Which brings us belatedly to the Omni Coliseum, a 16,000-seater venue in Atlanta, Georgia, in the early spring of 1991. Onstage are the support band, a feisty quintet celebrating their first hometown gig after months on the road across America. And the singer is mouthing a rap which he's repeated, more or less identically, night after night since the last time they were in Atlanta. Gesturing to the Miller Lite beer logos that litter the stage, he announces:

"You're not watching TV now. This is rock'n'roll, and there's not going to be any commercials. Except this one: here's my three-minute commercial

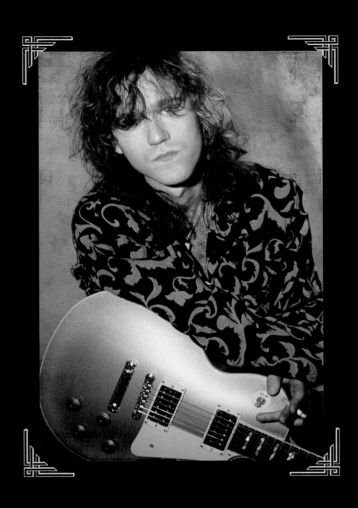

It was The Black Crowes, but it could have been any young band with a head full of ideals. If outspokenness was the only issue, then Chris Robinson could be any headstrong street-punk. But there is more to The Black Crowes than taking a stand for free speech and hippie values.

At the time of the ZZ Top débâcle, The Black Crowes' début album, 'Shake Your Money Maker', had already sold two million copies during a fifty-week run in the US charts. It's since doubled that score, with the follow-up, 'The Southern Harmony And Lyrical Companion', hard on its heels. Initially dismissed as clueless revivalists of the Seventies, rock's least street-credible era, The Black Crowes are now recognised as the latest inhabitants of the music's great tradition — toting a brand of blues and soul-soaked rock'n'raunch that leans and builds on Robert Johnson, Muddy Waters, The Rolling Stones, Rod Stewart and The Faces, Otis Redding, The Allman Brothers Band, Humble Pie and Led Zeppelin. They've single-handedly restored the glory of Southern rock, another Seventies leftover which had long since fallen into disrepair. And for graduate students of internal group dynamics, they've unearthed a classic love and hate fraternal conflict to place alongside any of the great creative powerplays of the past — Mick and Keith of the Stones, Ray and Dave Davies of The Kinks, Page and Plant in Zeppelin, Axl and Slash in the Roses, even the dreaded Rod'n'Ron in The Faces.

Influences are there for any self-styled critic to pull out of the air, but the Robinsons have — perhaps not surprisingly — begun to rebel against being caricatured as revivalists. When their first album appeared, they were pleased to take their place in rock's evolutionary chart, their Sixties and Seventies inspirations a far cry from the clichés of their hard-rock rivals.

After a second set of media comparisons for 'The Southern Harmony And Lyrical Companion', the children have started to deny their parentage.

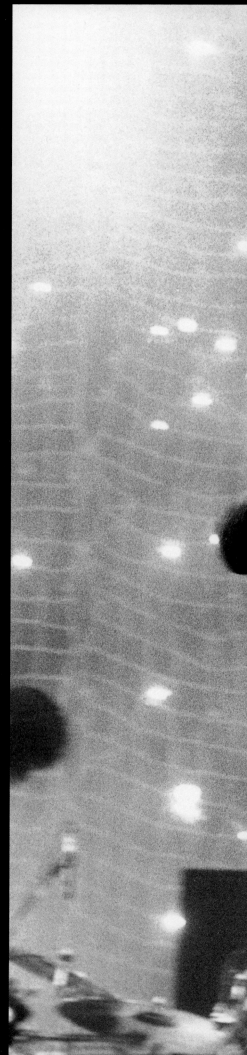

Rich Robinson concurred — albeit, as usual, in a different interview, this time with *Guitarist*:

"I'm baffled by the Stones and Faces thing. I mean, on our first record, the press didn't hit on what we were trying to do, and then on this record they're miles away again. For them to say either of the records sounds like the Stones or The Faces is insane. There might be bits of those bands in there, as far as influences go — music I've heard — because all the music I've ever heard is obviously an influence. You can only be influenced by the past. But this whole retro-Rolling Stones bullshit, I think it's just the journalists' way to get uptight and be lazy, picking up on what other people are saying rather than actually thinking for themselves. I don't think they really want to listen. There's so much music that we've heard throughout our lives that it all shows up as an influence. So why don't these guys forget about the influences and worry about what we're doing and what we actually sound like?"

He has a point. When the Stones themselves emerged out of the Dartford Delta in the early Sixties, they made no secret of their Chicago rhythm and blues lineage; but no hip young gunslinger from *New Musical Express* or *Melody Maker* was there to accuse them of ripping off Muddy Waters and Chuck Berry. As far as the Stones were concerned, they were simply repaying their influences by educating a new generation into the

joyous noise of Chess R&B.

Thirty or so years on, rock can't escape from its heritage. An industry has grown up around this most ephemeral of art forms, peopled by journalists who make a career out of piecing the uneven tapestry of popular music back into some kind of historical sense. And it's evasive, maybe even deceitful, for the Crowes to deny their musical roots. Rich Robinson may deny that his regular use of the Keith Richards patented open-G guitar tuning is in any way inspired by the Stones' mainman, but the path between master and devotee is too clear to miss.

But it's equally unrealistic to expect the Robinsons not to react when critics add up the sum of The Black Crowes' influences and assume they've fingered the entire content of the band. Everyone has influences, and some wear them on their sleeves more proudly than others. But almost every band — let's leave Bjorn Again and the Australian Doors out of this, OK? — brings something freshly-minted to their music. It's their distinctive choice of influences, of teachers, of heroes, that helps forge the identity of each new band: what matters isn't what they've been listening to, but what they make out of that input. The secret is to create something new, vital and alive out of the ghostly resonances of the past. That's something The Black Crowes have achieved on both albums — no question about it.

T he Black Crowes are a five-piece, but as you might already have gathered, their creative axis revolves around the brothers Robinson, Chris (born in 1966) and Rich (about three years his junior). Chris is the mouthpiece, any way you look at it — he sings, writes the lyrics and conducts the majority of the Crowes' interviews in an unstoppable flood of anecdotes, gripes, proclamations and put-downs. By contrast, Rich is quiet, almost withdrawn: when he speaks, he chooses his words carefully. He's the musician of the pair, though he's content to handle rhythm guitar onstage. He effaces himself so completely that the casual observer might imagine he was a non-contributing bystander of the creative process.

What sparks The Black Crowes is the relationship between these two, almost caricatured, individuals. As Rich Robinson told *Kerrang!* journalist Mick Wall,

"We're brothers, and deep down we love each other, but you'll find that on almost every issue, Chris and I completely disagree. We're like night and day,"

Chris concurred, in one of the rare interview situations where the brothers were prepared to share the same tape deck.

"The only thing we really come together on is the songwriting. Other than that, we fight all the time. I'm way less dramatic,"

Rich observes, in one of rock's great understatements.

"I'm more song-orientated, and he's more flaky-orientated."

If Rich is the band's craftsman, then Chris is the catalyst — the spark to the touch paper without which Rich would never have a jet-propelled vehicle for his creativity. Angular, with a voice that is sometimes reminiscent of

gangling comedian Emo Phillips, and a stage presence that is Jaggeresque in its confidence, Chris Robinson is the heart and soul of The Black Crowes. He feels every nuance of their music, and lives out the anguished uncertainty of their lyrics, on and off stage. Together, they fight — in the studio, on the road, even in front of a packed house. And from that conflict come songs that take age-old rock'n'roll clichés and revitalise them with the genuine breath of life.

The Robinsons were raised in Atlanta, the city which is the financial and spiritual centre of what is still optimistically known as the New South. The American Civil War ended nearly 130 years ago, with the Northern Union of States overcoming the Southern Confederacy after years of bloody and often gratuitously brutal conflict that pitted brothers and friends on either side of the ramshackle barricades. The official line is that the divisions which cut a jagged scar across the developing American nation — arguments about identity, about economic power, about national honour and most of all about the relationship between the black and

white races — have long since healed. That's the perspective of the prosperous cities of the American East Coast, however. Venture below the fabled Mason Dixon line into the heartland of the old Confederate Nation, and you can be forgiven for believing that the Civil War never actually ended, and is still being fought underground.

Like the eternal religious divide of Northern Ireland, the North/South conflict is imbued in children as soon as they're old enough to speak. To the North, the South is home to unapologetic racists and hillbilly farmers, fighting against progress in the name of naked prejudice. To the South, the North is a cruel, arrogant invader, determined to wipe out native traditions and promote the all-conquering advance of soulless modern technology. Southern kids grow up knowing that Northerners despise them: small wonder that sometimes they fit into the stereotypes created for them by the old enemy.

If you grow up in what feels like occupied territory, then you cling tight to your own native culture. In the Seventies, the music of the Confederate States was Southern rock — a hybrid of country blues, British R&B, Stax soul and Dixieland mentality which briefly threatened to become rock's common currency. Its founding fathers were The Allman Brothers Band, who whipped the essence of Robert Johnson's soul-searing acoustic blues into a wicked stew with Cream's instrumental pyrotechnics and the skin-tight soul rhythm of Memphis and Muscle Shoals. For two or three years, they were rock's cutting edge, and their majestic blend of improvisation and melodic flair spawned a host of imitators.

Foremost among them, and soon even more important in the Southern rock tradition, were Lynyrd Skynyrd. The Allmans never forgot that they were a blues band. Skynyrd exploded the genre barriers by inventing their own, where it was no longer possible to divide the complex set of musical influences one by one. Theirs was authentic Southern music, as rich, complex and doomed as the society which gave it birth. By the time that the original Skynyrd was decimated in the 1977 air crash that robbed them of their singer and leader Ronnie Van Zant, they'd become the blueprint for a generation of bands inhabiting Florida, Arkansas, Alabama, Georgia and Tennessee — names like the Marshall Tucker Band, .38 Special (led by Van Zant's brother Donnie), Dixie Dregs, Black Oak Arkansas and many more besides.

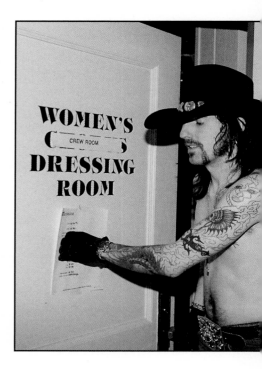

Ironically, the brothers Robinson didn't immediately latch onto the South's musical heritage. Even more ironically, the reason was that they believed what the rest of the world said about the South: the former nation was a land of rednecks, and therefore Skynyrd and the Allmans must be redneck rockers. Only in the late Eighties were they able to listen to their local musical tradition with open ears, and realise that, as Chris Robinson says,

"What Southern rock became is not what the Allmans started out to be. They were creating a new Southern sound. And what we do now is what I'd like Southern rock to become."

When The Black Crowes arrived with a début album soaked in generations of rock history, many critics questioned the authenticity of their vision. How could kids barely out of college have breathed in so much tradition in so short a time? What they didn't realise was that the Robinsons were raised on music.

"Dad was an actor,"

says Rich Robinson.

"He acted and danced off Broadway as a young person. He played semi-pro football and founded a rugby club. He's done a lot of things. There are a lot of different aspects to our family."

More importantly, their father, Stan Robinson, was a singer, who scored a small (No. 83) US hit in the spring of 1959 with the pop-rock novelty, 'Boom-A-Dip-Dip', on Monument Records — a single that, peculiarly, he doesn't seem to have bothered to follow up. He then mimicked the example of Bobby Darin by migrating from teenage ditties to the folk circuit, where he was also exposed to blues, bluegrass and country.

At home, Chris and Rich were able to feast on a musical diet that stretched from the cool New York jazz of Coltrane and Davis to the Irish folk of The Chieftains, via Muddy Waters' blues, Flatt and Scruggs' bluegrass and even the Woodstock-era rock of Joe Cocker.

"Chris and I developed an appreciation for music from our dad,"

Rich is quick to establish,

"because he liked everything from Harry Belafonte to Sly & The Family Stone. He never said, 'Hey, you guys have to listen to this'. It wasn't a forced thing. Both my mom and dad loved music and listened to it all the time, and because of that, Chris and I learned to like music as a whole. And that's the entire reason that we're here. We are influenced by good music, whatever it is, and whether it comes from 1890 or 1990."

No wonder that the boys grew up eclectic. Along the way, they picked up another set of influences from across the Atlantic — via the Stones, The Faces and Humble Pie, the last of these providing Chris Robinson with a vocal model in the shape of the late great Steve Marriott. And like every other would-be rock star of the Seventies, Chris was entranced by Steve Tyler of Aerosmith, who had the same effect on bedroom-mirror stage-strutters as Presley and Jagger did on previous generations.

With a father who had tasted the distant tang of fame, it would have been natural for the senior Robinsons to push Chris and Rich gently towards a career in music. But Rich is insistent that there was no hint of coercion:

"I taught myself to play the guitar. Dad never took an interest in Chris and myself being musicians. He never tried to force the issue. It was, 'If you guys want to do it, you can do it; whatever you decide to do, I'll be behind you, but I don't want to push you either way because you're individuals.'

Even young people have ideas and can make up their own minds, and he didn't want to tell us what he thought we should do because it was our lives, and he realised that. I just wanted to play guitar for whatever reason. It wasn't because I saw some guy and said, 'Hey, he gets a lot of girls', or I saw some guy and said, 'Man, I want to be him', because there's no-one on earth that I want to be. I just loved music, and that was the way that I wanted to express myself — and still do."

While Chris's vocal influences were easy to hear, and easy for him to assimilate, playing the guitar had to become a vocation for the younger brother. The Keith Richards influence has already reared its head — enough said on that subject. Rich Robinson, meanwhile, singles out the doomed acoustic troubadour Nick Drake, a finger-picking guitarist better known for his tortured, self-analytical and eventually despairing lyrics than for his undoubted instrumental prowess. After Drake, the influences become more obvious — Jimmy Page, Muddy Waters' remarkable slide playing, the obscure blues tunings of Mississippi Fred McDowell, and more recently, the inventive but powerful playing of Joe Perry from the original line-up of hard rockers Aerosmith.

By the time that the Robinsons elected to take up music as a serious option in the early Eighties, punk and new wave had effectively wiped out the Southern rock tradition as any kind of artistic force.

"In the mid and late Seventies, I think the music industry dropped the ball,"

Rich Robinson opines,

"and I think that's why there was rarely a good band around in the United States in the Eighties. There was just this huge low in music. It was a sack of shit. I think money became too important. Disposable bands came in and out, and people became TV stars rather than rock stars. There was no mystery to bands any more."

Closer to home, the outlook was no more promising.

"When we started getting out there in the clubs,"

Chris recalls,

"Atlanta was a very 'alternative' town. Now, with the benefit of hindsight, it's possible to realise what the alternative movement

did. It affirmed the right of everyone not to be able to play. It was almost bad to be able to play your instrument. If you mentioned Aerosmith or AC/DC to anyone, they would pull a face. Simplicity is a cool thing, but you have to take it somewhere. It's just like the blues: how many times has a band gone out there with the same chord progression? Is that fun? Does it really mean anything any more? So the music we played wasn't very alternative at all, but we still felt much more comfortable playing our own thing, rather than

trying to fit in with anyone else's idea of what we should be doing."

Georgia's musical pioneers in the early Eighties were R.E.M., and their crossover success on the national and then international stage predetermined that the State's bands had to adopt a jangly, alternative edge if they wanted to thrive.

Chris and Rich Robinson began gigging in 1984 as Mr Crowe's Garden - a title taken from a favourite children's story, with the extra 'e' added to the crow as a gesture of solidarity with the then-flourishing Paisley Underground bands who had sprung up alongside R.E.M. Starting out with a memorable gig in Chattanooga, Tennessee - their first paycheque bounced - Mr Crowe's Garden mixed covers of songs by Love, the Velvet Underground and even Led Zeppelin with original material in the R.E.M. tradition. Even in their mid-teens, the Robinsons were fanatical about their music, so they shed accomplices on a regular basis. Their original drummer, a cousin, lasted only a few months; he was replaced by one Jeff Sullivan, who in turn left them for a rival outfit called Drivin'n'Cryin'. Drummer number three was Steve Gorman, pinched from another Atlanta combo, Mary My Hope, with whom the Crowes shacked up for several months.

When journalist Chris Nadler noted that several of the Robinsons' short-term musical cohorts from these years had since crawled into the spotlight to criticise the brothers, Rich's response was philosophical enough:

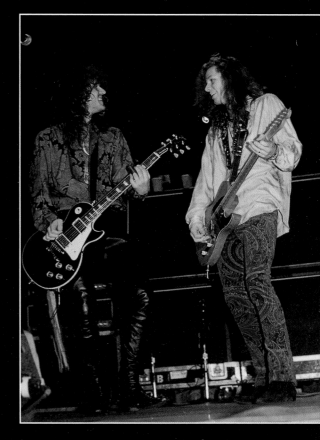

"That's always going to happen, isn't it? If I played with Chris and Rich Robinson for four months one time and I'm still just another musician making pizza or tending bar and never had the commitment or foresight to stay involved with this, well, I'd be bitter, too. Having a day job sucks - I've had them. But these people talk about these 'times' as if they were something special. I just remember being fucking miserable and wasted drunk, just because we wanted to be in a band and do it for real. We didn't want to go about it half-assed."

By 1986, Mr Crowe's Garden had become The Black Crowes - under which guise they were asked to cut a demo for the local representative of A&M Records, who'd caught wind of the growing vibe about the Robinsons' potential. The offer found the group in their customary situation of being between bassists, so the one-song audition tape (of a number called 'It's Not Fair') featured a session man who had little affinity with these cocky teenagers and their glory dreams.

"Everyone resented us,"

Chris recalls,

"and thought we were little brats."

A&M HQ in California weren't impressed, but it was another of the company's A&R men, George Drakoulias, who seized the opportunity. In an episode already translated into legend, Drakoulias ventured into an Atlanta outlet of Kentucky Fried Chicken, and asked one of Colonel Sanders' staff who was happening in town. He recommended the Crowes, and so Drakoulias caught up with the band on one of their first visits to New York. He was taken less by the forced 'new wave' feel of their music than by Chris Robinson's natural class as a frontman: only when he spoke to the band did he discover that the Crowes themselves were pursuing a musical direction against their artistic inclinations. He took them into a local studio for a week to allow them room to develop and arrange their own best material, but

then couldn't persuade his bosses to take the plunge. Drakoulias called in the band, and said he was moving to California and leaving A&M for a smaller label. Were they prepared to wait until he was settled, on the promise of a recording deal? Chris had only one question:

"Do we get to make the record we want?"

And the contract was settled on a handshake there and then.

It was mid 1989 by the time that Drakoulias's new role at Def American Records - launched by Rick Rubin, former pioneer of the rock/rap crossover at the vital Def Jam label - allowed The Black Crowes to cut their début album. They joined a roster of bands like Danzig, Wolfsbane and Slayer - one-dimensional speed merchants marketed as prophets of doom and devilry. That wasn't The Black Crowes' style at all. The 'Shake Your Money Maker' album was a stunningly mature set of recordings which was at once retrospective in its feel, and utterly contemporary in its sonic quality and relationship with the outside world.

After five years of personnel changes, the band had become a five-headed union of resources and skills. The Robinsons were still in charge, of course, with Steve Gorman on drums, bassist number six Johnny Colt, and second guitarist Jeff Cease (a refugee from a Nashville band called Rumble Circus). The quintet shared a meagre $5,000 advance - which they paid off as soon as the world at large caught wind of the record. In an era when even the most rebellious rock bands seemed to have been assembled by marketing executives, the Crowes were a blast of cool air. You could pick out their influences from the back of the largest stadium, but hadn't that also been the case with their predecessors, like Zeppelin, the Allmans and the Stones? What the Crowes offered was majestic guitar riffs, tightly constructed rock songs that reeked of traditionalism, and lyrics that revived timeless themes - the tortured collapse of romantic illusions, the devil's choice between selling out and surviving, the nagging angst of the idealist in an age of compromise. Best of all, there wasn't a sample of a synthesiser in earshot: with The Black Crowes what you heard was what they were, with no apologies asked or received.

The album took a while to break through, but regular rock-radio exposure for tracks like 'Jealous Again', the anguished crawl through 'She Talks To Angels' and the supercharged cover of Otis Redding's 'Hard To Handle' - allied to word-of-mouth reports from those who'd seen the Crowes live - gradually brought the band to the masses. Meanwhile, the

Chuck Leavell played on the record and did a really good job. But, like, what about the songs? So we went out on the road for the first year after that to demonstrate that we didn't really need keyboards. I can stomach those comparisons with the Stones for maybe one or two articles, but then it gets redundant and old. I can understand critics trying to find parallels, but there's so many fucking, stupid-ass labels in music. Music isn't about narrowing things down. If anything, it's always been about

record reached Britain in March 1990, eliciting instant comparisons with fly-by-night Faces revivalists The Quireboys, and hard rockers like Thunder.

In the States, the comparisons weren't that subtle. Those open-tuned chords, that microphone strutting, a five-piece - it had to be the Stones, right? Inadvertently, the Crowes didn't help matters by recruiting an occasional Stones sideman to play on their record.

"When 'Money Maker' first came out,"

Rich Robinson recalls with a sigh,

"a lot of people zoned in on the fact that Chuck Leavell was on it. Of course, most fucking critic assholes have to find an angle. All right, so

widening perspectives. I feel like telling the critics, 'When have you been on tour for 20 fucking months? And when have you had to listen to assholes like yourself? How about if I critique your syntax?"

Without keyboards available to flesh out the sound on stage, everything fell back on to the guitars. And Rich Robinson and Jeff Cease renewed an honourable rock tradition - following in the footsteps of that five-piece English band whose name we're not allowed to mention - of breaking away from rigid distinctions between lead and rhythm guitar parts.

"Some people ask me why I don't play solos,"

Rich says,

"but I'm not 'the solo guy' because I think a good song is much harder to come by than a good solo. A great solo could be in a shitty song and who

would give a shit? But a hack solo in a great song - it's still a great song. It's harder to be a rhythm player than it is a soloist, because anyone can make their fingers move really fast and play shitty solos. It's much harder to know when to back off, to know when not to play rather than when to play. It's so easy to overplay. And so many people still don't understand that."

Though 'Shake Your Money Maker' won fine reviews in Britain, for the moment The Black Crowes concentrated on promoting the album at home. 'Jealous Again' won heavy MTV video play in April -

"There are no naked women or shit in this clip,"

Chris boasted.

"It's a performance video because that's what the band does best. Our priorities do not hinge on money and videos of tits and ass."

"Videos are here to stay,"

Rich added,

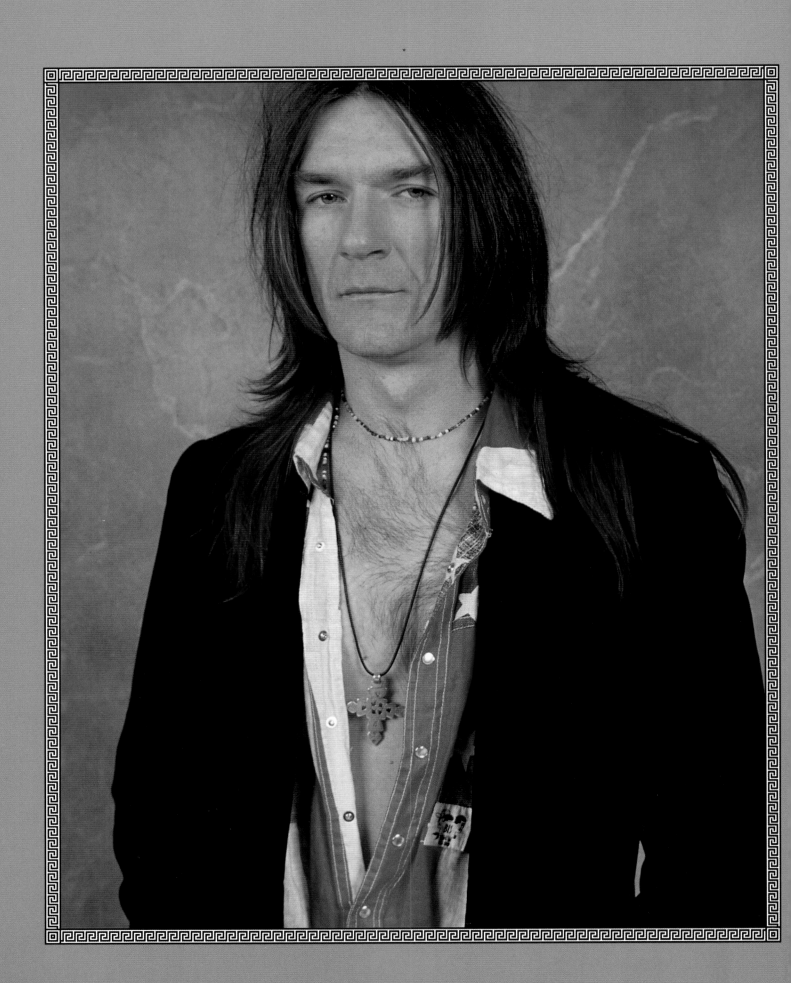

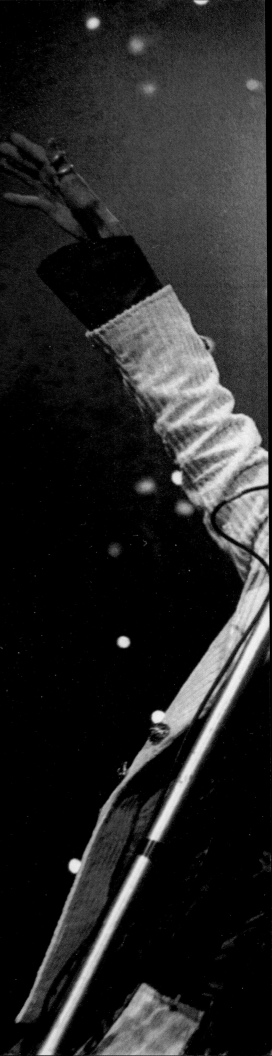

"whether they're ruining the industry or not. And I think that instead of sitting round and bitching about them, which you can do, it's better to try to take more of an interest, because if you're a creative person, you can make creative videos."

Meanwhile, the Crowes were out on the road, sharing the bill with another tip for the top, Junkyard.

"It's sexy and funky and intense,"

Jeff Cease beamed midway through the six-week tour which ended at the Omni club in Oakland.

"Being on the road is the most fun we have." And already the band were looking ahead to their next album, previewing up to six new songs a

night, the best received of which was entitled 'Kick The Devil Out Of Me'

("Something people say to each other in the South," Chris Robinson explained).

Then, on June 7, the band played their first British date, at the famous (if not quite original) Marquee Club in London. They headlined a handful of club dates, and then supported Dogs D'Amour at larger venues in Glasgow, Nottingham, Manchester and back in London at the Astoria. The British media were impressed - mildly - and concentrated on comparing Chris with Mick Jagger, fuelling another set of stories complaining that the Crowes were simply a retro outfit.

After a week or so break, they were out on another package - this time playing arenas behind their early heroes, Aerosmith. The combination wasn't a coincidence: Aerosmith mainmen Steve Tyler and Joe Perry had asked for them.

"The biggest thing in the world for me is if I gain the respect of another musician,"

Chris said in a daze,

"especially one who you've listened to and learned from since you

first started playing guitar. Joe Perry saying he was knocked out with our album, that just makes our year!"

This being The Black Crowes, the Aerosmith tour wasn't entirely without incident. Chris Robinson:

"One radio station refused to play our music because I refused to answer his stupid questions. I don't see why I should have to be nice to some local DJ. So I walked out. He eventually played the record anyway."

And so the year went on, one concert jaunt succeeding another, and each one upping the band's profile and sales figures. There were gigs behind another hero, Robert Plant; more new songs entering the set, like 'Miserable' and 'Shake 'Em On Down'; even a painfully slow odyssey through The Beatles' 'Get Back' as a sop to those journalists who were stuck on the 'revivalists' theory. As 1990 ended, and another tour - the ZZ Top ticket -

loomed, Chris Robinson looked back over The Black Crowes' year:

"The last twelve months have been like Sodom and Gomorrah on five dollars a day."

At least 1991 would bring them a pay-rise.

In January, Chris was still full of enthusiasm for the upcoming record, with sessions scheduled for that Spring:

"It's shaping up pretty good. The songs I've written are head and shoulders above 'Money Maker'. That's natural, really, because we're still developing as songwriters. It'll be mellower, but the songs will be nastier. The grooves will be funkier. I want it all to be melody-

orientated. I'd like to record some jam sessions as well, to keep it fresh."

That seemed to cover most bases.

Sure enough, the band's next move was funkier, and nastier - but no way was it mellow. The ZZ Top tour ended in the minor fracas mentioned earlier. The Crowes then set out on a headlining tour, which rapidly ran into chaos when they sacked their support act, the ill-fated Maggie's Dream, when Chris Robinson discovered the naughty boys had recorded a Miller Lite radio commercial.

"You want to sign commercials, then go join a jingle house,"

Robinson nagged. The replacements were an Atlanta band called Uncle Green, who not only got paid for appearing with the Crowes (rather than having to pay for the privilege, as most top bands insist in these autocratic days) but were also allowed assistance from the headliners' lighting and sound crews.

More controversy ensued, as Chris supposedly spat at a girl in a 7-11 store in Denver, and was then arrested for stealing two cans of beer which his roadie had already bought. Threatened with further charges of assault and disturbing the peace, Robinson eventually managed to convince the forces of law and order he was no

budding Charles Manson, but the farcical nature of the incident testified to the increased tension surrounding the band. In retrospect, Chris regretted the incident - less for what it was than for what it became:

"The people who are into The Black Crowes and who buy Black Crowes records are into it because of my singing. The people who get their records for free write about me spitting on an obnoxious person in a 7-11. If more critics knew what The Black Crowes were about and were into that, they'd recognise what I do as a vocalist. But you rarely read about that."

At the end of their tour in June 1991, the Crowes flew their logo-covered flag at half-mast atop Tower Records' Sunset Boulevard store in LA -

"In mourning for the death of rock'n'roll,"

according to Chris. There were manifestos, as well - one stuck to the side of Tower, exhorting its readers to "Wake up, try and remember a time before you believed everything you've seen or read," the other outside each venue on the tour, proclaiming: "The Black Crowes have NO association with any venue sponsors, so feel free to put all your attentions to having a good time. Peace & Soul, The Black Crowes."

From LA, the band flew to London, ostensibly to attend the Third International Rock Awards ceremony in London - a vain attempt by the rock community outside the States to rival the prestigious Grammy Awards shindig. The ceremony may have been meaningless, but the Crowes hadn't flown six thousand miles just to hang out with the rest of the rock aristocracy in dinner jackets. They won the Artist of the Year and Album of the Year categories - proof that their album sales had won them respect from their peers. While in London, the band performed for free in front of an invited audience (they had no work permits, so they weren't able to charge for admission) at Ronnie Scott's. Playing an entirely acoustic set, with full-time sideman Eddie Harsch on piano, the band were introduced by Chris rasping,

"Welcome to a few songs filled with jet lag and alcohol abuse,"

and then proceeded to trip through a ragged but often fiery set that included yet another batch of new material ("You're Wrong", which inspired Led Zeppelin comparisons, "Thorn In My Pride" and the tongue-in-cheek "Darling Of The Underground Press"), an elongated version of the untitled blues that had ended the first album (now called "Live Too Fast And We're Gonna Play It Now Blues"), and even a cover of Ry Cooder's acoustic blues epic, "Boomer's Story". And then the jet lag and alcohol took control, as Chris Robinson collapsed backstage, and had to be hustled to the nearest quack, who pronounced a severe case of exhaustion after almost 18 months of continuous roadwork.

Still there was no new album. Instead, the band returned to the States, and then flew back to Europe in August for the Crowes to open the Monsters of Rock festival at Donington. This wasn't one of their career highlights, either for the band, who were disheartened by the narrow musical horizons of most of the audience, or the crowd, who had their worst suspicions about the Crowes fulfilled when they came onstage to the sound of James Brown's "Sex Machine". Funk music? What was that doing at a metal gig? So much for the musical melting pot theory of modern rock. The Crowes tossed their heads and flew home - only to return one more time for their fullest U.K. tour to date.

By now, the exhaustion and ennui were beginning to show. Their London gig at the Town & Country Club was a sell-out, but the band never caught fire. Bristol was a rare moment of inspiration, but the Birmingham show was a drag, although archivists did note that the band included a cover of the Allmans' standard 'Dreams' for the first time. And in Edinburgh, Chris Robinson and Jeff Cease ended up trading insults and blows with the audience. The Crowes were relieved to leave for Japan, knowing that the next stop was Atlanta, where Rich Robinson could have his niggling stomach pains attended to, and the band could finally work on the second album.

Before they left for home, Chris Robinson noted that their début record

"has nothing to do with The Black Crowes right now. I really love the songs, and I'm proud of it - your first record is like your first kid - but we're in a much different place now. We're really turned on, we're hitting on some really solid, heavy things. We've already got the next album written, but who knows, we're gonna keep writing, and we might even dump the stuff we've got now."

And the effect of touring?

"This band always knew that it was going to take going on the road for two years to sort of cut ourselves from the cocoon, to be something else. That's what it is, really, it's a metamorphosis.

Sometimes it happens for people, sometimes it doesn't. I would like to think that as far as the musician-ship goes, there's only been an improvement.

"From the touring, I learned that I never wanted to grow up and be like one of those people who throw in the towel. And I learned that I never want to become jaded."

After nearly two years of waiting for the time to make the record, the Crowes knew exactly what they wanted to do. Living on Rock Star Time, 'Recording An Album' is supposed to take a year: the Crowes taped and mixed theirs in three weeks, the actual recording taking just eight days. Eddie Harsch (or Hawrysch, as they now insist on spelling it) remained on board for the entire project, lending his experience earned from backing blues masters like Muddy Waters and Albert Collins; while a local church choir added depth and colour to a couple of tracks. And the Crowes eschewed digital recording - of course - in favour of the traditional values of the analogue sound.

"We recorded this record in eight days, because we can,"

Rich Robinson boasted.

"Why would you need three years to make a record? If that's the case, then you're not a band. People might call me an asshole for saying that, but I think it's cheating the kids and the fans who go out and spend money on a record, who spend their time following a band and respecting and loving that band. For the longest time everyone thought that people in bands were puppets and idiots. But then again there haven't really been any bands that have said what they felt in a long while."

Speaking to the American magazine *Guitar World*, Robinson expanded the point:

"How long does it take to go, 'All right, let's try this amp'? You plug it in and say, 'It sounds cool but it needs a little more treble. All right, that's done.' We did the basic tracks live and overdubbed the percussion and the layered guitars. Marc played his track, which was the solo and his part. And I played my main rhythm part, then overdubbed acoustics, like on 'Hotel Illness' and 'Bad Luck Blue Eyes'."

Wait a minute - who's Marc? Well, with The Black Crowes, a little conflict was only to be expected. Guitarist Jeff Cease didn't survive the pre-production period, and was ousted in favour of Marc Ford, formerly with power trio Burning Tree. Industry rumours had it that Izzy Stradlin - recently departed from Guns N' Roses - nearly took the job. And although producer George Drakoulias lasted long enough to finish the album, he had parted company from the band by the time it was released in May 1992. In future, it seemed, the Crowes would be producing themselves.

So what happened with Jeff Cease? Rich Robinson explains:

"When we did the first record, I was 19 - I'd graduated from high school the year before and was living at home with my parents. And I

wasn't that good a player - I'd only been playing three or four years. But after two years on tour and all the experiences we had, I think the four of us had reached a different level. Jeff Cease didn't, and that's why we needed someone new."

"The Crowes were my friends,"

Marc Ford adds.

"It was like coming in and jamming with some pals. But I'd only heard these songs a dozen times, while we were putting them together in Chris and Rich's garage. We made up the parts as we recorded them, and we

watched each other to see a new change coming while we were recording the song. It wasn't possible to pre-think anything at all. The record is kind of uneasy and aggressive - it's the whole idea of learning a shitload of things in three days, recording on the fourth day and then finishing in eight. Your instincts are fully working, whatever you do. You can't second-guess yourself. You just go by instinct and jump in head first."`

Rich Robinson is eager to dispel any ideas that, for the Crowes, recording is simply a matter of reproducing what they do on stage:

"To me the studio is a totally different entity.

You can't go on stage and try to re-create your record, because it's boring. I mean, your record is for sitting at home and listening to, and live is for taking it somewhere different. We don't really jam in the studio: we just go and record the songs. And that's how I write songs. I like flowing things, things that flow together and make sense. I like doing things that mean something. Some come whenever they come for whatever reason, and I never ask myself what they were about - I just wrote them. I think if you start analysing it or trying to think back to

how or why, or questioning why it happened, you start worrying about whether it's going to happen again, and then it won't happen."

Named and fashioned after an ancient hymnbook, 'The Southern Harmony And Musical Companion' was packaged like an exotic cousin of the Stones' 'Exile On Main Street', all circus freaks and shadowy, stark photography. And the music matched the mood of the artwork, sacrificing some of the swagger of the début album for a savage, often chilling atmosphere of emotional and spiritual realism that led to more comparisons with Jagger and Richards' 1972 epic. At the centre of the album was 'Thorn In My Pride', with a lyric that confronted all the "angels" and "devils" who were competing for the soul of the band. As another key song put it, 'Sometimes Salvation' was at hand; sometimes the Crowes seemed about to slip into 'Hotel Illness'. Either way, the band were airing their traumas and triumphs in public.

After the album came the public exhibitions - an appearance on the MTV Music Awards, where they opened up TV coverage of the show, and managed to outplay Nirvana

without even dreaming of trashing their equipment. At least the Crowes came away still respecting Nirvana, unlike some of their fellow billtoppers. Rich Robinson:

"You have these bands like Def Leppard - I'm sure they're the nicest guys in the world, but I was at the MTV Awards when they were trying to do a soundcheck, and they couldn't do a song because their tapes weren't working. And they couldn't sing a ballad in the key that they recorded it because of some studio trick! What is that? That's not a band! What do you say to someone like that?"

MTV was fast becoming a second home for The Black Crowes, in fact they stripped down their sound to appear on the acoustic-centred 'Unplugged' show in the autumn of 1992, and also ended up hosting one of the cable network's regular rock shows. Then it was back on the road, for the slyly named 'High As The Moon' tour - without, you can be certain, any tapes masquerading for live performances.

"You paid money to see a band,"

Chris says in disgust at the idea.

"The guys in a band that are using tapes must be having a shit horrible time to get up there and smile and move their mouths along to a tape. Why are you there? Why don't you go and work for the fucking Post Office if it's a job for you? These are the guys who go backstage and say, 'Where's someone to blow me? And how many T-shirts did we sell?' I like honest people."

For the moment, Chris adds,

"We've put ourselves in a position where no-one tells us what to do. We've really taken great strides to remove ourselves from these other entities who start telling you how you should look and what you should be. We look around and usually think, 'What can we do that no-one else is doing? What is really going to be us?' I don't think we need to be anything we're not. That's never really been an option for us."

"I think the only reason this band is a phenomenon is that we're not mainstream,"

Rich Robinson reckons.

"We're one of the only

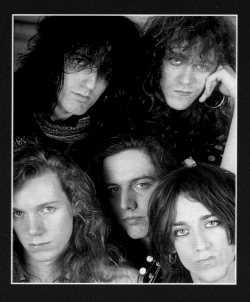

bands in a long time to sell as many records as we have without really having Top 40 support. In the industry, that makes us a phenomenon. But you have to accept that people in the industry are going to try to use that and try to turn it around into, 'Hey, The Black Crowes are pretty smart guys, they came up with this whole 'real' thing. That's a good move. They sold some records out of that. Let's try that.' In the meantime, we'll go wherever we want to go. We have control of where we're going. The only thing that could warp the way the band goes is the media, because they lie, for the most part. They come up with their own reasons and their own interpretations, and people just believe what they read."

That's why Chris Robinson refused to have his face alongside his brother's on a *Guitar World* photo-spread, as he reckoned that Rich should be the sole focus of attention in a guitar magazine; and why he says that he may stop giving interviews entirely:

"The day's gonna come when I don't want to communicate any more, except about the music."

And it's why, according to the band's self-imposed reality rule, the Crowes may disintegrate at any time, if the feeling and the motivation disappears, as Chris is determined to point out:

"It may all be over tomorrow. I may get on this tour and not even have a feeling for it any more. The whole point is

that we don't do this for other people. I don't do it to pay Def American's phone bill. I could have found something easier to do instead."

Rich touches on some of the other pressures surrounding the band, like the prevailing atmosphere at the major American record labels -

"It's just business now, and a lot of people out there who work for these record companies are idiots who know nothing about music" -

and Top 40 radio -

"I don't think they give a lot of bands a fair shake; those guys have been spoon-feeding this pure shit to their audience for so long."

So success hasn't transformed The Black Crowes from idealists into careerists. It's difficult for any rock artist to maintain enthusiasm for their music and faith in their principles in the face of the many tantalising temptations of the rich and often corrupt modern music business. But the Crowes are determined to put up a fight. If in twenty years' time, they're out on the oldies circuit, bashing out pale imitations of their long-dead hits for a middle-aged audience, then they will simply have followed the same dingy path as too many of their predecessors.

Most likely The Black Crowes won't survive that long - long enough, anyway, to sacrifice everything for the evil lustre of the greenback dollar. There's too much energy, passion and commitment in the band for anyone to predict a safe and settled future. But if the explosion comes, it will be glorious to watch. And it will leave behind a catalogue of music - two albums, to date, but maybe more if the Robinsons can keep their unstable balancing act on the rope for another few years - which will outstrip 99.9% of the sound committed to tape in the name of 1990s rock. For the moment, they're averaging two out of two: even for a band as cocky as The Black Crowes, that's not bad.

The Black Crowes *Discography*

SINGLES

Jealous Again / Thick'n'Thin
Def American DEFA 4 (7") April 1990

**Jealous Again / Thick'n'Thin /
Waitin' Guilty**
Def American DEFA 412 (12")
April 1990

**Jealous Again / Thick'n'Thin /
Waitin' Guilty**
Def American DEFAC 4 (CD)
April 1990

**Jealous Again / Thick'n'Thin /
Waitin' Guilty**
Def American DEFAP 412 (12" picture
disc) April 1990

Hard to Handle / Jealous Again
(acoustic)
Def American DEFA 6 (7") July 1990

Hard to Handle / Jealous Again
(acoustic)
Def American DEFAM 6 (cassette)
July 1990

Hard to Handle / Jealous Again
(acoustic) **/ Twice as Hard** (live) **/
Stare it Cold** (live)
Def American DEFA 612 (12")
July 1990

Hard to Handle / Jealous Again
(acoustic) **/ Twice as Hard** (remix)
Def American DEFAC 6 (CD) July 1990

Hard to Handle / Jealous Again
(acoustic) **/ Twice as Hard** (live)
Def American DEFAP 612 (12" picture
disc) July 1990

Twice as Hard / Jealous Again
(live)
Def American DEFA 7 (7") April 1991

Twice as Hard / Jealous Again
(live)
Def American DEFAM 7 (cassette)
April 1991

Twice as Hard / Jealous Again
(live) **Jealous Guy** (live)
Def American DEFA 712 (12" poster
sleeve) April 1991

Twice as Hard / Jealous Again
(live) **Jealous Guy** (live)
Def American DEFAC 7 (CD)
April 1991

Twice as Hard / Jealous Again
(live) **/ Could I've Been So Blind**
(live)
Def American DEFAP 712 (12" picture
disc) April 1991

**Jealous Again / She Talks To
Angels**
Def American DEFA 8 (7") June 1991

**Jealous Again / She Talks To
Angels / She Talks To Angels** (live)
Def American DEFA 812 (12" with free
patch) June 1991

**Jealous Again / She Talks To
Angels** (live) **/ Could I've Been So
Blind** (live)
Def American DEFAC 8 (CD)
June 1991

Jealous Again (acoustic) **/ She
Talks To Angels** (acoustic) **/
Waitin' Guilty / Strutting Blues**
Def American DEFAP 812 (12")
June 1991

Hard To Handle / Sister Luck
(live)
Def American DEFA 10 (7")
August 1991

Hard To Handle / Stare It Cold
(live)
Def American DEFAP 10 (shaped
picture disc) August 1991

Hard To Handle / Dreams (live) /
Stare It Cold (live)
Def American DEFA 1012 (12")
August 1991

Hard To Handle / Sister Luck
(live) / **Stare It Cold** (live)
Def American DEFAC 10 (CD)
August 1991

**Seeing Things / Could I've Been
So Blind**
Def American DEFAC 10 (7")
November 1991

Seeing Things / Jealous Again
(live) / **Hard to Handle** (live) /
Twice As Hard (live)
Def American DEFA 1312 (12")
November 1991

**Seeing Things / Could I've Been
So Blind** (live) / **She Talks Angels**
(live) / **Sister Luck** (live)
Def American DEFAG 1312 (12")
November 1991

**Seeing Things / Hard to Handle /
Jealous Again / Twice As Hard**
Def American DEFAC 13 (CD)
November 1991

**Remedy / Darling Of The
Underground Press**
Def American DEFA 16 (etched 7")
May 1992

**Remedy / Darling Of The Under-
ground Press / Time Will Tell**
Def American DEFA 1612 (12" in
circular tin) May 1992

**Remedy / Darling Of The
Underground Press / Time Will
Tell**
Def American DEFCD 16 (CD)
May 1992

**Sting Me / Rainy Day Women
Nos. 12 & 55**
Def American DEFA 21 (7")
September 1992

**Sting Me / She Talks To Angels /
Thorn In My Pride / Darling Of
The Underground Press**
Def American DEFCD 21 (CD)
September 1992

Hotel Illness / No Speak, No Slave
Def American DEFA 23 (7")
November 1992

**Hotel Illness / Words You Throw
Away / Rainy Day Women Nos.
12 & 55**
Def American DEFX 23 (12" clear vinyl
with 1993 calendar) November 1992

**Hotel Illness / Rainy Day /
interview with Chris Robinson**
Def American DEFCD 23 (CD)
November 1992

**Hotel Illness / Words You Throw
Away / interview with Rich
Robinson**
Def American DEFCB 23 (CD in box)
November 1992

ALBUMS

Shake Your Money Maker
Twice As Hard / Jealous Again / Sister
Luck / Could I've Been So Blind /
Seeing Things / Hard To Handle /
Thick n'Thin / She Talks To Angels /
Struttin' Blues / Stare It Cold
Def American 842 515 March 1990

**The Southern Harmony And
Musical Companion**
Sting Me / Remedy / Thorn In My
Pride / Bad Luck Blue Eyes Goodbye /
Sometimes Salvation / Hotel Illness /
Black Moon Creeping / No Speak No
Slave / My Morning Song / Time Will
Tell
Def American 515 263 May 1992